DATE DUE

It's My Body ABC

Lola M. Schaefer

Heinemann Library
Chicago, Illinois

© 2003 Heinemann Library
a division of Reed Elsevier Inc.
Chicago, IL

Customer Service 888-454-2279
Visit our website at www.heinemannlibrary.com

Designed by Sue Emerson, Heinemann Library; Page layout by Que-Net Media
Printed and bound in the United States by Lake Book Manufacturing, Inc.
Photo research by Jennifer Gillis

07 06 05 04 03
10 9 8 7 6 5 4 3 2 1

Library of Congress Cataloging-in-Publication Data
Schaefer, Lola M., 1950-
  It's my body ABC / Lola M. Schaefer.
      p. cm. – (It's my body)
Includes index.
Summary: Photographs and simple text depict parts of the body and related concepts, from "Ankle" to "Zzzz."
  ISBN 1-4034-0894-7 (HC), 1-4034-3481-6 (Pbk.)
  1. Body, Human–Juvenile literature. 2. Alphabet–Juvenile literature. [1. Body, Human. 2. Alphabet.] I. Title.
II. Series: Schaefer, Lola M., 1950- . It's my body.
  QM27 .S37 2003
  611–dc21

                                2002014738

Acknowledgments
The author and publishers are grateful to the following for permission to reproduce copyright material:
pp. 3, 5, 6, 7, 10, 12, 13, 14 Brian Warling/Heinemann Library; p. 4 Custom Medical Stock Photo; pp. 8, 18 Robert Lifson/Heinemann Library; p. 9 Greg Williams/Heinemann Library; p. 15 Kevin R. Morris/Corbis; p. 16 Joe Sohm/Chromoshm/Stock Connection/PictureQuest; pp. 17, 19 Digital Vision/PictureQuest; p. 20 Collection CNRI/PhotoTake; p. 21 Owaki-Kulla/Corbis; p. 22 Lee White/Corbis; p. 23 row 1 Brian Warling/Heinemann Library; row 2 (L-R) Custom Medical Stock Photo, Brian Warling/Heinemann Library, Brian Warling/Heinemann Library; row 3 (L-R) Brian Warling/Heinemann Library, Brian Warling/Heinemann Library, BSIP/PhotoTake; row 4 (L-R) Brian Warling/Heinemann Library, Custom Medical Stock Photo; back cover Brian Warling/Heinemann Library

Cover photographs by Brian Warling/Heinemann Library

Every effort has been made to contact copyright holders of any material reproduced in this book. Any omissions will be rectified in subsequent printings if notice is given to the publisher.

Special thanks to our advisory panel for their help in the preparation of this book:

Alice Bethke, Library Consultant
Palo Alto, CA

Eileen Day, Preschool Teacher
Chicago, IL

Kathleen Gilbert,
Second Grade Teacher
Round Rock, TX

Sandra Gilbert,
Library Media Specialist
Fiest Elementary School
Houston, TX

Jan Gobeille,
Kindergarten Teacher
Garfield Elementary
Oakland, CA

Angela Leeper,
Educational Consultant
North Carolina Department
of Public Instruction
Wake Forest, NC

Some words are shown in bold, **like this.**
You can find them in the picture glossary on page 23.

A a Ankle

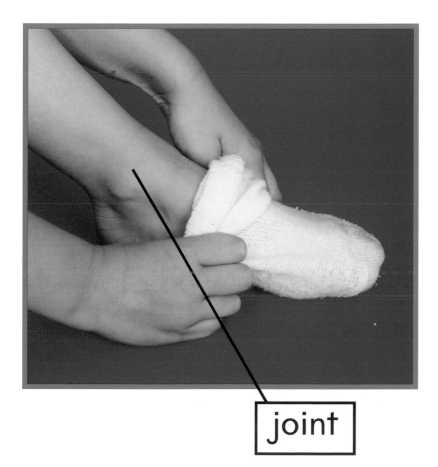

joint

The **ankle** is a **joint**.

It helps you twist and turn your foot.

B b Bone

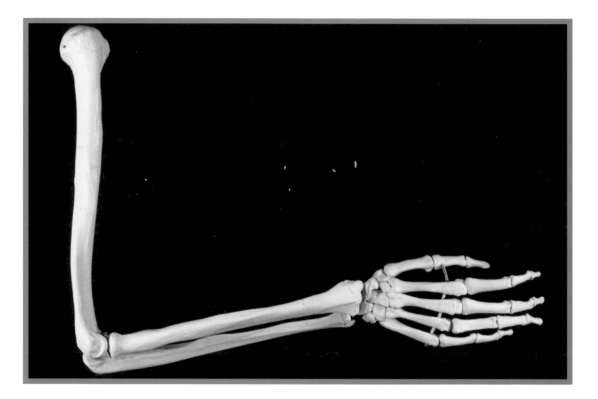

Bones give your body its shape.

Bones get longer and harder as they grow.

C c Chin

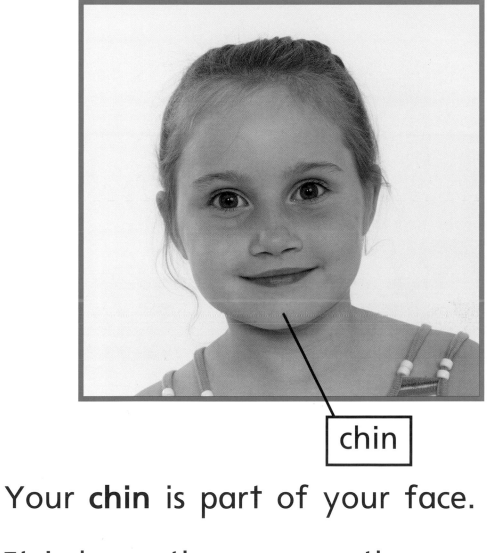

chin

Your **chin** is part of your face.

It is beneath your mouth.

D d   Dimples

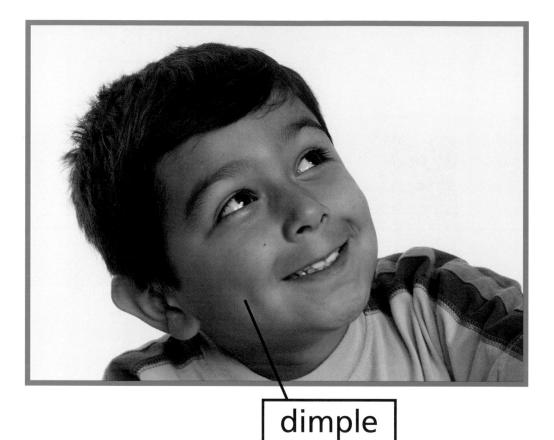

dimple

Muscles help people smile.

Some people have **dimples** when they smile.

E e   Elbow
F f   Finger

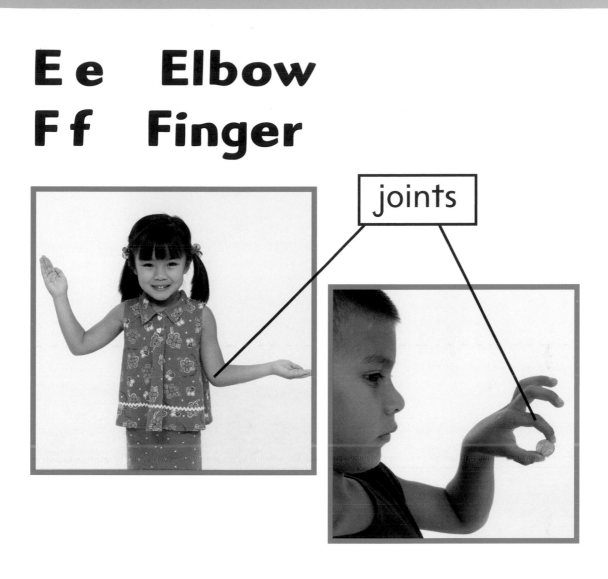

joints

Arms bend at the **elbow**.

Fingers bend at **joints**.

G g   Grown-up

Grown-ups' bodies are big.

Grown-ups are taller than children.

H h Hair

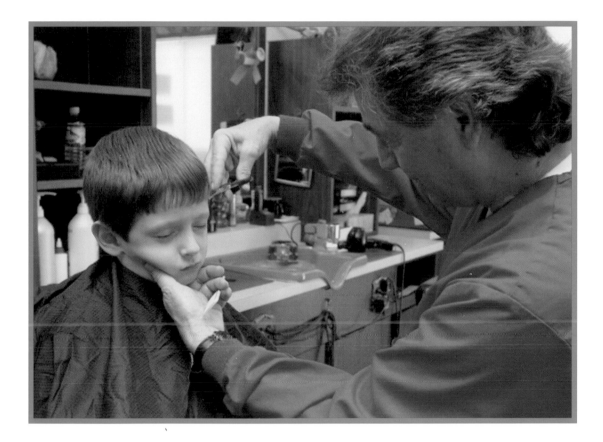

Your hair grows every day.

If you didn't cut it, it would grow very long.

I i Iris

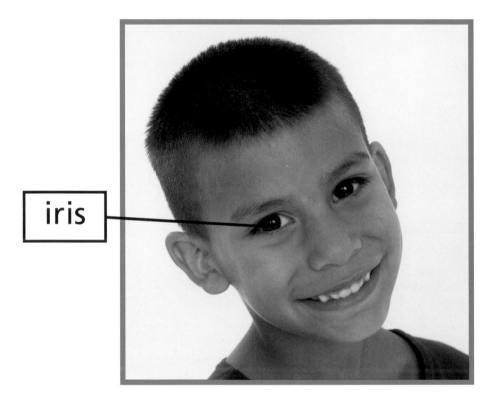

iris

The **iris** is the colored part of your eye.

It can be blue, brown, green, or gray.

Jj Joint
Kk Knee

knees

Bones meet at **joints**.

Most joints can bend, like these **knees**.

Ll Leg

Legs help you move from place to place.

Your legs help you dance.

M m   Mouth
N n   Nose

You can open your mouth wide.

Or you can wiggle your nose like a bunny.

O o   Open
P p   Pupil

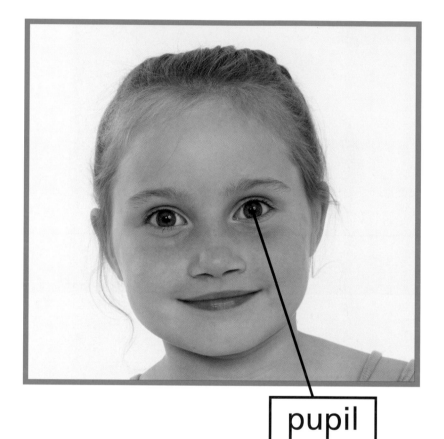

pupil

Pupils are holes in your **irises.**

They open to let light into your eyes.

Q q   Quiver

Your skin quivers when you are cold.

Your **muscles** shake to make you warmer.

R r Run
S s Slide

Legs help you run.

Your legs help you slide into home plate!

Tt Toes

Toes help you stand and walk.

Toes help your feet grip.

U u V v
Ultraviolet Rays

Sunglasses help keep your eyes safe from **ultraviolet rays.**

Ultraviolet rays come from the sun.

W w Wrist

Your **wrist** helps your hand move up, down, and around.

Your wrist is a **joint**.

Xx X Ray

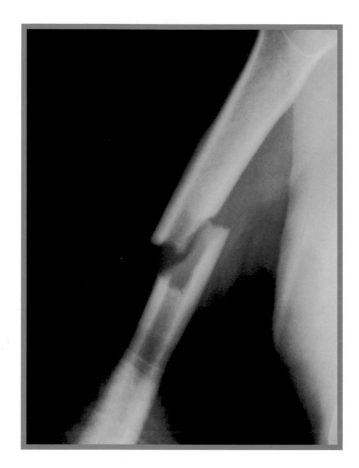

X rays take pictures of **bones.**

This bone is broken.

Yy Yawn

This baby is yawning.

Muscles pull your **jawbone** open when you yawn.

Z z   Zzzz

You need a lot of sleep to keep your body healthy.

Zzzz ... good night!

Picture Glossary

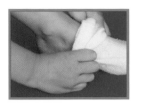

ankle
page 3

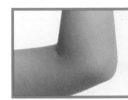

elbow
page 7

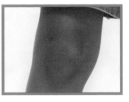

knee
page 11

ultraviolet rays
page 18

bone
pages 4, 11, 20

iris
pages 10, 14

muscle
pages 6, 15, 21

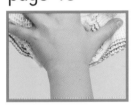

wrist
page 19

chin
page 5

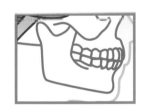

jawbone
page 21

pupil
page 14

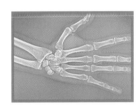

X ray
page 20

dimple
page 6

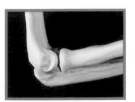

joint
pages 3, 7, 11, 19

Note to Parents and Teachers

Using this book, children can practice alphabetic skills while learning about parts of the body. Together, read *It's My Body ABC*. Say the names of the letters aloud, then say the target word, exaggerating the beginning of the word. For example, "/r/: Rrrr-un." Can the child think of any other words that begin with the /r/ sound? Try to sing the "ABC song," substituting the *It's My Body ABC* alphabet words for the letters a, b, c, and so on.

Index